ADULTING MADE EASIER POCKET GUIDE

160+ Ways Millennials Can Navigate Love and Relationships Today

Nathan Smith

© **Copyright 2021 - All rights reserved.**

The content contained within this book may not be reproduced, duplicated or transmitted without direct written permission from the author or the publisher.

Under no circumstances will any blame or legal responsibility be held against the publisher, or author, for any damages, reparation, or monetary loss due to the information contained within this book, either directly or indirectly.

Legal Notice:

This book is copyright protected. It is only for personal use. You cannot amend, distribute, sell, use, quote or paraphrase any part, or the content within this book, without the consent of the author or publisher.

Disclaimer Notice:

Please note the information contained within this document is for educational and entertainment purposes only. All effort has been executed to present accurate, up to date, reliable, complete information. No warranties of any kind are declared or implied. Readers acknowledge that the author is not engaged in the rendering of legal, financial, medical or professional advice. The content within this book has been derived from various sources. Please consult a licensed professional before attempting any techniques outlined in this book.

By reading this document, the reader agrees that under no circumstances is the author responsible for any losses, direct or indirect, that are incurred as a result of the use of the information contained within this document, including, but not limited to, errors, omissions, or inaccuracies.

TABLE OF CONTENTS

Dating 101

Breaking Up or Letting Go

General Relationship Advice

Friends/Family While In a Relationship

Money In A Relationship

Being Single

DATING 101

<1>
If You're Going To Be Late, Please Call

It's not only important to let someone know you're running late but also why. If the issue is something out of your control, make sure they know that and offer an alternate plan if it's possible or just try to be on time from there on out.

<2>

What It Means When Someone Says: "I Want You."

To say 'I want you is not always about romance - it could also mean wanting someone's company, attention, skills/expertise, or time." The person wants to be with you and wants to spend time with you.

<3>
Ask Someone Out This Week

It's OK to be nervous when asking someone out, but if you don't ask them, then they're never going to know the answer. "If you want a relationship and are interested in this person," says Loeschner, "then go ahead and ask."

"Be open with who you are, what your life is all about. You have nothing to be ashamed of."

<4>
Don't Put Yourself in the Friend Zone.

The friendzone is a place where you're friends with someone, but not in a romantic way. If you don't feel like they are interested in being more than just friends, it's time to move on and find somebody else who reciprocates your feelings.

<5>

Be Present In Your Dates

If you're not fully present on a date, it will probably end up boring and not go well. It helps if both people are invested in the conversation or activity happening at that moment.

<6>

Don't Date Someone You're Not Crazy About

Dating is an emotional process that should be taken seriously. If you're not feeling it, then don't go on a date because you'll only end up hurting yourself and wasting your time.

<7>
Don't Kiss and Tell

It's not cool to go around and tell everyone. You're better off keeping that information private because other people may find out in a way that feels uncomfortable for them.

<8>

What To Do In Your Dating Profile

Your dating profile should be a representation of who you are. It might take some time to get it right, but your future dates will thank you for the effort invested.

<9>
How To Deal With Flirting

If someone is flirting with you and they're not your significant other, don't worry about it too much because that is a sign of flattery.

<10>
Don't Talk Wrong About Your Previous Partners

When talking to your current partner, you shouldn't talk about bad things in the past. That doesn't mean they won't happen again, and it's not fair for them.

<11>
Don't Assume You're Exclusive With Your Partner.

If you want to be sure that your partner is exclusive with you, make them say it. You should talk to them about this, and if they refuse, then the relationship might not work out.

<12>
Don't Just Date For Looks

Just because someone is good-looking doesn't mean they will be a great partner. Even if your relationship starts as physical, you should try to have other things in common. Emotional connection is essential.

<13>
Dating Profile Picture

Close-up pictures of your face are the best type because it's easier to see all of you. Ensure that there is a good balance between light and dark so everything can be seen in detail, but not too much contrast, or your photo will look flat and unnatural. Also, make sure to have enough headspace around you for people to know what you look like overall.

<14>
Show The Real You In Pictures

Don't just show pictures of you smiling and looking at the camera. Show things that are uniquely you, like your favorite hobby or travel destination.

<15>
Understand Ghosting Won't Be Your Fault

Many people think if they were only better looking, wiser, funnier, etc., they wouldn't be ghosted. It's not you. It's about them. If they're not interested, it's their loss and your gain.

<16>

Open With A Specific Unique Compliment

It's effortless to develop something that stands out and will make the person you're chatting with feel good.

<17>

Use Puns When Saying Hello In Your Dating App

If you don't like the person's name or photo, this is an easy way to break the ice. Just don't be mean about it.

<18>
Be More Than Just A Pretty Face

Offer something of value to the other person. Let them know what you're into, and let it be known that you like their interests too (even if they don't). It's OK to say, "I love your taste in music!" even if they haven't mentioned anything about their love of music.

<19>
Stop Dating and Commit

This might sound silly, but if you are in a relationship for more than two years without dating anyone else, stop using your dating app profiles. You're already committed!

<20>
Be Mindful of Grammar When Messaging

If you're not a native English speaker, try to avoid using too many abbreviations and phrases that sound like they could have come from another language. People are quick to judge, unfortunately.

<21>
Start a Video Date

If you're looking to make a connection with someone, try video chatting via Skype or FaceTime. It's the best way of seeing how they are animated and their body language!

<22>

It's Socially Acceptable To Use Dating Apps Now

It's been a long time since people have used dating apps in secret. If you're going to use them, just make sure the rest of your social media is squeaky clean and that what you put up on Tinder isn't all about drinking at bars

<23>

Have Fun on Bumble and Tinder!

You are supposed to have fun too! If you're feeling good about the match, it's OK if they don't respond immediately or at all. Take a break from swiping for a bit.

<24>

Who Pays For The Date?

If you were a girl, would the guy always pay? No, it's up to whoever asks.

<25>
Always Wear Protection

Just because you're in a relationship, it doesn't mean that you can stop using protection. If your partner isn't on birth control and doesn't want to wear condoms with each other, then the adult thing is for them to get tested.

<26>
After The First Date

After the first date, it's time to find out if you want this person in your life. But some questions will answer whether or not you should continue with them until they're a long-term relationship partner.

These include:

- How did I feel when we were together?
- Did my initial feelings after meeting and spending time with them change after the date?
- Did I think any spark in the conversation with them when we were together?
- Did they make me laugh and smile a lot more than usual?
- Did they show up on time to our meeting spot, or did I have to wait for them before anything could happen?

<27>
Don't Date Married People

It's best to stay away from married people because they are not fully committed. They may have a family at home, but that doesn't mean you should be their second option, or worse yet, the only option for them.

<28>

Date Someone Emotionally Mature As You

It's important to date someone who is as emotionally mature as you are. Someone who can understand your emotional needs and meet them adequately will make for a healthier relationship in the long run.

91) Dating and Rejection come hand in hand

Dating is all about the process of rejection. It's how we learn who likes us and who doesn't, but it can be challenging to deal with when you want someone, and they don't feel that way back.

<29>
Meet Somewhere Public

It's always a good idea to meet somewhere public at first when meeting someone new. If you spend time with them initially, it will be easier to get an idea of who they are as a person and if there is any chemistry between you two.

<30>
Don't Flake But Communicate

If you are going to flake on someone's date, do it before the day so they can find a way to fill their time. It is not cool, and it will make them think less of you if they have made plans with other people.

<31>

Walk of Shame Doesn't Have To Be Shameful

If you're at the point in your relationship where you are spending nights or days with someone, don't let a walk of shame make you feel bad about yourself. Don't be ashamed and just go on with what's next for that day.

<32>

Don't Get Drunk on the First Date

If you're going on a first date, try to keep it light and not too heavy. Try activities such as walking around the city or playing cards instead of getting drunk.

<33>
Coffee Dates are a Safe Bet

A coffee date is a perfect way to get to know someone without the pressure of having to sleep together on the first night. It's also great for people who don't drink or would rather stay sober.

<34>
Don't Be Afraid To Be Goofy and Genuinely Express Yourself

It's essential to have fun and enjoy life with your partner, even if it means embarrassing yourself.

<35>
Be Open-Minded

Being in a relationship doesn't mean you always agree on everything. It takes patience and understanding to come to the best solution when both parties disagree over something.

<36>
Don't Ignore Red Flags

Red flags are essential and need to be on your radar. Suppose you're constantly feeling unhappy in your relationship. In that case, it's time to take a step back and reevaluate what is going on.

<37>
Don't Date People That are Mean To Waiters

You may think this is a joke, but it's not. If you're in a relationship with someone who treats waiters poorly or doesn't tip them well, they most likely treat other people harshly too. This will make your life much more complicated if the person you love is mean to others daily.

<38>
Don't Box Yourself In

Don't box yourself in with limiting beliefs or relationships that will not allow you to grow as an adult. You should constantly be evolving, and being open to new possibilities can lead to the best outcome. When it's time to find love again, don't settle for less than what you deserve.

<39>
First Impressions Lasts

First impressions are important because they last. When you first meet someone and don't have any preconceptions of who they are, it's less likely that your first impression will be skewed by their past relationships or lousy eating habits.

<40>

It Might Not Work Out- But You'll Be Better Off For Trying

You should try anyway because even if it doesn't work out, it's a lesson learned, and you'll be better off for testing.

<41>
It's OK To Be Vulnerable

Vulnerability can be strength! It shows that you're comfortable enough to show who you are. Being vulnerable is a sign of courage and bravery.

It can be scary to put yourself on the line, but it's rewarding when you take the risk.

<42>
Make Time For Your Relationship

It may sound counterintuitive, but couples need some "me" time as much as they do together time. This is because relationships are all about balance: The more you give your attention and love to yourself, the more you'll have to give your partner.

<43>
Be Honest with Yourself and Others

Being honest about who you are, what you want, and how you feel is a crucial part of being an adult. This helps relationships because if something isn't working for either person, it can be addressed without going on indefinitely or becoming more severe than necessary.

<44>

How To Have Uncomfortable Conversations

It's not easy to have a difficult conversation, but it can be necessary. If you don't address the issue early on, then things will only get worse and more complicated as time goes by

<45>
If you find someone who interests you, message them!
Don't wait!

You don't want to seem too eager, but there's nothing wrong with being proactive in reaching out!

<46>
Decide on a Budget on Dates

Pick an amount that will work for both of your wallets, and don't spend more than what you decide upon!

<47>

Write a Good Bio That Will Attract Someone of Interest

It's not a secret that people check up on your social media to find out what you like, so make it easy for them!

<48>

If They Respond To Your Message, Be Polite

Don't be too forward, and don't rag on them about their interests. Be professional in your response!

<49>
The Second Date Should Be Outside!

You don't want to be cooped up in a restaurant for the whole date. It's better to get out and explore or just go on an adventure together with your significant other!

<50>
When To Call Them After A Second Date, Don't Overthink It

If it was a night that you both enjoyed, and they made some effort to contact you, then don't hesitate. Text or call them the next day!

If he doesn't text back after calling him, wait at least 24 hours before testing again

It might be more of an issue on their end than yours. They could have bad cell reception, or something happened with their car.

<51>
What To Text If You Want To See Them Again and They Don't Respond

If the person you're seeing doesn't respond to your text, send them a friendly reminder that they were supposed to see you in 24 hours. Tell them how much it would mean to see them again and express some of their qualities about why you like spending time with him/them.

<52>

Ask Questions, But Not Too Many Either

If they don't want to answer your questions, then it might be because they don't feel comfortable with you and do not trust you. Don't ask too many personal questions because the other person will think of them as an interrogation.

<53>
Asking Them To Be Exclusive with You

Being exclusive is a big step in any relationship. It's essential to be sure with your decision because it could cause some serious problems if you're not ready for this commitment.

Don't rush into exclusivity unless you are 100% sure that's what you want and know the benefits of being committed exclusively versus simply dating someone casually.

BREAKING UP OR LETTING GO

When it's time, move on from your partner.

It may seem like a lot of hard work, but after some thought, you'll realize that it may be the best option for both of you. You may have found someone else, or maybe you need some space to find yourself again.

It's OK if a relationship ends because two people just weren't meant for each other.

It can be hard to understand and accept that the love was not strong enough between two people, but sometimes it is better after time has passed. Don't be sad that it ended; smile that it happened and you learned to love someone else.

<54>
When You Need to Break Up With Your Partner, This Is How To Do It

Sometimes relationships aren't working out, and one or both people need to break up. If you're in this situation, don't try to end things yourself because it will only cause more problems than necessary - work with your partner to have a mutually amicable breakup.

<55>

How To Know When You Should End A Relationship

An excellent way to know when you should end a relationship is to evaluate the common sense problems. This has nothing to do with what's happening in your life. Still, instead, it focuses on how you feel personally.

<56>
How To Get Out Of A Relationship

The only way that you can get out of an unhealthy romantic or non-romantic relationship is through standing up for yourself and your needs. If you don't end it, then the person will continue to take advantage of you until they're satisfied or there's nothing else they can get from you.

<57>
How To Deal With A Breakup

A breakup can be hard on anyone, but the difference between people who get over one quickly and those who are still grieving months or years later comes down to how healthy their relationships were before the breakup.

<58>
Don't Break Up Over Text

Breaking up over text is a crappy way to go about it. It's cowardly and immature.

<59>

Don't Rush To Find Someone Else After A Breakup

It's natural to be eager for a new relationship after your breakup. But don't rush into it, or you'll end up with someone who is not correct. Give yourself time to heal.

<60>
Put In The Time and Effort On Yourself Before You Get Back Out There

If your partner has broken off their relationship, then this can lead them to feel distracted from

<61>
Heartbreak Is Inevitable

It's something that everyone goes through, and unfortunately, it can't be avoided.

It would also be great to have some time away from the person so you could rebuild your life with new friends or hobbies and establish a sense of independence before jumping back into another relationship without any boundaries at all.

<62>
Break Up Like A Grown-Up

This can be the most challenging part of relationships because it's not a simple "we're over." Breaking up is hard enough, but when you have to do it yourself, that makes things even harder.

That being said, breakups should always be done with respect and love for the other person to make sure they don't feel like crap.

<63>

Understand Your Love Language

This is a great way to make sure your partner knows how you like to be loved and vice versa. Understanding this will help the both of you know when each other needs love or for their love language to be fulfilled. This can also lead to some fascinating discussions about why they feel that way and what makes them happy, which in turn should bring you closer together.

<64>

Don't Compare Your Relationship To Others

This one is huge because it can lead to a negative cycle when you compare relationships to others.

Not only does this make your partner feel like they aren't good enough, but it also makes them not want to share with you their problems or what's on their mind for fear of criticism from the other person.

<65>
Avoid Being Gaslighted

Gaslighting is when one partner wants the other to question their reality. This might be as simple as not calling someone back, or it could get worse with more serious things like mental abuse and even physical violence.

<66>

Don't Let Your Relationship Become A Competition

Competing in relationships can lead to some unhealthy habits that are hard to get back from break. Whether it's who makes more money or how much harder you're working than the other person, this type of behavior can lead to some unhealthy habits.

<67>
Put Yourself First Sometimes

Everyone in a relationship must take time to themselves and find what they love about themselves, so they don't feel like their partner is smothering them in the relationship.

<68>

What If They Don't Want To See You Anymore

If the person you're seeing doesn't want to see you anymore, do not push them. If they say no, they don't want to be with you and if they ignore your texts, leave them alone because they are likely thinking about returning to their old life.

GENERAL RELATIONSHIP ADVICE

<69>

Communication Is Key

It's important to always communicate with your partner. Even if you're in the same room, it doesn't mean that they're paying attention. That might be a good time for you to take a walk and talk about things that are bothering you so that they can understand where you're coming from before more severe problems arise.

<70>
Make Time For Each Other

It's essential to make time for each other, even if it means taking a break from doing what you're doing. You have to learn how to balance all aspects of your life. The relationship stays strong and doesn't fall apart because one person was too busy or forgot about their partner.

Don't forget: communication is critical.

<71>

Put In The Work To Create A Happy Home Together

An adult in a relationship needs to put in the work required for their home with their partner even if they're not always around as much anymore because of other responsibilities at work, school, and life in general.

<72>

Be Supportive Of Your Partner And Their Goals

You have to be supportive of your partner and their goals. You must keep up with what they're doing, even if it doesn't seem like something exciting or worth following, because when the time comes for them to need support from you - whether it is emotional support or physical support-you'll be there.

<73>

Being Open To New Things Is Always Important

It's essential to be open to new things in a relationship so that you can both grow and learn. If one of you is closed-minded, it'll stop the other person from increasing as well.

If some people are just not cut for relationships or they're too tied up with their own life at this stage- which is entirely understandable - then it's OK to let them go.

<74>
Remember That You're Not Perfect, But Try Your Best To Be Honest With Yourself About What You Need From This Relationship

You're not perfect. No one is. But it's essential to be honest with yourself about what you need from this relationship-whether which means talking more about your feelings or taking the lead in a fight.

It's also essential to have an open conversation about boundaries and lie for both people involved in the relationship.

<75>
How To Be A Good Partner

This is something we all want to be, but it's not always easy.

It can seem like there are a million different things you need to do, but doing any of those minor tasks for your partner says so much about how much they mean to you.

So it's the little things that we need to work on and make an effort to do.

It's the little things that can sometimes mean so much.

<76>
Be Patient With Your Partner, Especially During Tough Times

It's essential to listen and be present with your partner by just being there for them, and they will love you even more because of it.

<77>
Be A Good Listener

Sometimes listening is more than half the battle.

And it's essential to be a good listener because your partner might not always feel like they can talk about their problems with you. Still, if they know that you are there and willing to listen, then they will open up even when it feels hard for them.

It's OK to have your own opinion but share it when the time is right.

<78>
Share Responsibilities, Not Just Chores But Emotional Needs As Well

If you have a partner, split up the duties and share them. For example, suppose one is in charge of doing the grocery shopping. In that case, they can also cook dinner while their partner does house cleaning every other week or something like that.

Be willing to take on specific tasks so your relationship lasts longer than it would otherwise.

<79>

Remember That You Are Not Entitled To A Partner's Time

This is a hard lesson to learn, but it's essential. It can be easy for people in relationships to feel like they're entitled to their partner's time and attention all the time because of how much they invest into them - both emotionally and physically.

But remember that you are not your partner's slave or servant; if your relationship is based on mutual respect and communication, then you should have a say in what happens too.

If your partner doesn't respect that boundary and tries to guilt-trip you for not being available all the time just because they want it, then maybe they're not worth your time or effort at all.

<80>
When Something Bothers You, Don't Let It Simmer And Talk About It

Let your partner know as soon as possible so that you can work it out together.

Do not let things get to a boiling point where they erupt and cause unnecessary issues between the two of you.

<81>
Be Honest With Yourself About What Makes This Worth Relationship Fighting

You can't fight for yourself and them if you don't have the energy.

Suppose it makes you feel resentful or unhappy. In that case, that's not fair to anyone involved and needs addressing immediately because this is supposed to be something happy for both of you.

<82>
Have Your Own Life Outside Of Them

Sometimes people find themselves in relationships where they're completely consumed by their significant other. Don't lose your identity.

Suppose you don't have friends outside of your relationship or activities that make you happy on your own. In that case, it's time to reevaluate what you need to add back into your life.

<83>

Don't Lie About Who You Are In The Name Of Love

Stay true to yourself. You're not going to change for anyone.

This is the person who you chose to spend the rest of your life with, and they should love all parts of you: flaws included.

<84>
Be Honest About How You Feel

If something's bothering them or makes them happy, let each other know in a way that feels comfortable so you what to do and not do in a relationship.

<85>
Make Sure The Relationship Is Making Both Of You Feel Fulfilled

Your wellbeing depends on your happiness and vice versa if one person is constantly unhappy in a new or old relationship - that says something about them more than it says about you.

<86>
Give Each Other Space When Needed To Figure Out Things Alone

Suppose you're both stressed or not in a great place. In that case, it's important to give yourselves the time and space they need without pressuring them into talking about what's bothering them. Listen intently but don't push for answers if they aren't ready yet.

<87>

Tell Them How Much You Love Them Every Day

Not many people do this enough, but it's important to tell your partner that they make a difference in your life and appreciate the things they bring into it. It's not always easy being with someone who is emotionally unavailable or has difficulty expressing their feelings, so it's great to know that they are loved.

<88>
Show Affection With Physical Touch

This is an important love language for many people. Couples need physical touch to feel loved, so it's essential for them to display affection in private and public.

<89>
Keep Your Promises

This is a little thing that can go such a long way. Just remember, don't make promises you can't keep or break the ones you already have. People will remember you this way.

<90>
Don't Spend All Day On The Phone or Computer When You Have A Partner

It's essential to spend time with people in person. If you have a partner, make sure that they know how much you care and love them by spending quality time together!

<91>
Dealing With Jealousy In Relationships Is Normal, But Don't Let It Consume You

Jealousy is a very normal feeling because of all the love and emotions that one can have for their partner. What's important here is not to let jealousy take over your life or make decisions for you!

<92>
It's OK If Relationships Aren't Perfect; Nobody Expects Them To Be

Nobody expects you to be perfect, but you should do your best, so don't expect to be with someone perfect either. You two should work together on the relationship and understand each other to grow as a couple!

<93>
Speak Your Mind And Be Honest

It's essential to allow the person you love to know what they mean to you and let them speak their mind. Suppose there is a disagreement or misunderstanding between either party. In that case, it should always be resolved so that no feelings are hurt, and both people feel loved.

<94>
Different Types of Relationships You Can Have with Someone Else

One can have many different types of relationships with someone else, including platonic friendships and romantic relationships. What's important to know about these various connections is that they all require work to be successful. It would help if you had a good working relationship and understand how each person will handle the other ones'.

<95>

Make Them Feel Special When They Don't Expect It

The best way to keep a relationship going is by making them feel special when they don't expect it. This means that you should try and do something nice for your significant other without expecting anything in return.

<96>

Handle Disagreements With Your Partner

You'll run into conflicts with your partner, and sometimes you'll disagree about how to handle them. You mustn't believe this means the relationship is doomed - disagreements happen in almost every healthy couple.

<97>

What It Means When Someone Says: "I Love You."

You will find people who are saying 'I love you for different reasons - some may be making an excuse, others might mean that they care about them in general." There are many ways of showing you love them, and everyone is different. Find out what your

partner likes and wants to hear.

I love you can be a compelling phrase, but it means different things for everyone. Some people say "I love you" as an excuse because they don't want to commit or they are scared of commitment, while others may mean that they care about them in general."

<98>

How To Commit To A Long-Term Relationship

If you are thinking about committing to a long-term relationship, then both of your expectations must match. You might want to rethink the idea if one person wants children while another doesn't or if one is looking for something serious and the other wants no strings attached."

<99>

What To Do If Your Partner Is Too Protective Of You

There is a time and place to protect your partner, but it can be a problem if they're always watching over you. They need to understand that being in a relationship means giving and receiving love."

<100>
Be Honest And Open With Your Partner(s)

It is essential to be honest with your partner about what you want from the relationship when things are going well to meet those needs as much as possible.

<101>
Do Things Together And Apart

Do things together and apart. Relationships are about having a life partner, but it is also essential to maintain your own identity. If you do not have outside interests, this will lead to boredom in the relationship, which can cause resentment or feelings of being trapped.

<102>

Relationships Require Work, Never Forget That

If you don't have to try, then the relationship has already failed.

<103>
Don't Try To Change Your Partner

Don't try to change your partner. If you do, it will not work, and they may resent that you are trying to mold them into what you want them to be.

<104>
Don't Stay In Your Relationship Just Because It's Emotionally Convenient

Emotional convenience leads to complacency, which will eventually lead to the end of the relationship anyway.

<105>

Don't Hold Grudges

It's only going to make you feel worse than the other person. Just let it go and move on.

<106>
Don't Expect A Relationship To Solve Your Problems

Relationships are challenging work, so don't expect them to solve your problems for you.

<107>

Don't Judge Your Partner's Past

You don't know what their life was like, so try not to judge them.

<108>
Don't Be Afraid To Change

If you're in a relationship for a long time and find that things just aren't the same anymore, then it's OK to change. You won't be with this person forever, but at least you know you can evolve to something better.

<109>
Your Finances in the Relationship

Relationships are lovely, but they do come with a price. They require you to invest time in them and some of your money if you want the relationship to work out. Keep this in mind when deciding whether or not it's worth investing in someone else- is this person worth more than what I am giving?

<110>
Responsibilities In The Relationship

If someone is interested in you, then they should be willing to help contribute. If not, there might be a good motive behind that lack of interest, and it's best for both people if the relationship ends sooner than later.

Does this person seem more excited about our future together instead of focusing on the now?

<111>
Put Yourself First Once in a While

Adults need to put themselves first every once in a while because you usually put the other person first when you're in a relationship. That's what makes relationships work!

<112>
Maintain Your Self-Confidence

Sometimes, when we last, losing self-confidence can happen, and that is never productive for an adult or someone who wants to be in a healthy relationship.

<113>
Self Love is Everything

Love yourself first before bringing someone else into the mix. It is essential to know and love yourself before entering a relationship because it can be challenging for an adult to find someone who loves themselves as much as they do

<114>
Having Chemistry Is Vital

While there are many things to consider when being in a relationship, chemistry is one of the most critical aspects. If you have lost interest or don't feel it anymore, that doesn't mean you're done with that person entirely; however, breakups may be inevitable if they lack this aspect.

<115>
Trust Can Be Even More Important Than Love

Trust is the bedrock of any relationship. It would help if you had this for a healthy, functioning, and long-lasting partnership. Without trust, you're doomed from the start; it's not worth risking your happiness or even your life on someone who doesn't know how to be there for you in both good times and bad.

<116>
Don't Expect Them To Read Your Mind

It's essential to be clear about what you want in a relationship. If you don't speak up, your partner may not pick up on hints that you might have given out subconsciously and vice versa.

<117>

Don't Force Something That Isn't There

It's natural to want companionship and love. However, suppose you need a relationship because you're lonely or unhappy with your current life. In that case, it may be best to wait for the right person who can provide that unmet aspect of your life instead of settling for someone else.

<118>

Be Open With Them About What's Going On In Your Life

It will help keep the relationship fresh and exciting because they'll feel needed and wanted by getting updates from their significant other.

<119>
Secrets Are No Fun

If you keep things from them, it will make the person feel insecure or untrustworthy. This

may lead to problems in your future and should be avoided at all costs.

<120>
Set Boundaries Together

Boundaries are essential for any healthy relationship because they'll set expectations of acceptable behavior between both parties.

<121>
Keep Your Love Alive With Date Nights

Most couples go through periods of imbalance - one person may want more togetherness than the other, or one partner may feel neglected when they are home while their partner is at work all day. To maintain balance in relationships, ensure that both partners spend quality time together, whether this means going out for dinner or taking a walk around the block.

<122>
Have A Date Night At Least Once A Week To Keep The Spark Going

Date night is essential for any relationship because it'll bring the two of you closer. It's not about going to a fancy restaurant or expensive show; date nights should be fun no matter what you decide to do together as long as there are good intentions in place.

<123>

If There Are Kids Involved, Compromise!

Children have the power to change any adult-only plan into something that involves both parents. Be flexible with each other because children need their two parents around as much as possible.

<124>
It's OK To Disagree

Both sides of a relationship must have their voice heard. If you find yourself constantly on the same page, it may be because one side isn't speaking up or being listened to. Make sure your partner knows they are loved and listened to!

<125>
Put In The Effort

Yes, this needs to be said. It's one thing to love someone, but it takes a lot of work. If you're constantly feeling like your partner is doing more than you are for the relationship, ask them about their thoughts and feelings on how things are going.

<126>
Don't Give Ultimatums

Ultimatums are the death of relationships. If you feel like your relationship is on a downward spiral, then it's best to speak with them about how you think and what they can do to make things better for both of you. Ultimatums put people in challenging positions because there will be someone who ends up getting hurt either way.

<127>

Make Your Own Decisions, Even If They're Wrong

Don't let your fear of being wrong control how you live your life or who you love. You may make mistakes along the way, but it's worth it to forge your path.

<128>
Great Relationships Aren't Built In A Day

It takes time to get to know someone and be comfortable with them. Building trust, respect, and understanding can take weeks or months before you can feel like you're fully yourself around that person.

<129>
Become Best Friends With Your Partner

A relationship is a two-person team, and you'll both be better off for it. It's not always easy to communicate your feelings or thoughts--especially if they're hard ones! But the more effort you put in, the closer you'll become

<130>
Stick Up For Yourself

When someone close to us hurts our feelings, we usually try to brush it off because "it doesn't matter." But really, it matters even more. When you are hurt by someone close to you, your feelings should be validated. This is not a sign of weakness but rather a strength.

<131>
Know What Love Means To You

There's no right or wrong answer for this question - everyone has their idea about what love entails, and it can change as time goes on. So know exactly where you stand in terms of the type of relationship makes sense for yourself because relationships work when both partners agree on their parameters.

<132>
Be Honest With Each Other

Being honest doesn't mean being harsh, hostile, aggressive, or making assumptions without getting all sides of the story. Honesty just means giving an opinion while speaking from a place of respect and kindness.

<133>
Learn How To Do Things On Your Own

Don't depend solely on the other person because they start feeling like they need to take care of everything, which isn't suitable for anyone if taken too far and leads to a lack of independence.

<134>
Wait A Year Until You Cohabitate

It's essential to see how things go before committing. Even if you're in a relationship for years, it still might not work out, and this way, one person doesn't lose their home or have any shared assets with another person too soon!

<135>
Don't Make Excuses For Your Partner When They're Acting Up

This is one of the most important things you should do in relationships. You need to have a conversation with them and tell them what's wrong instead of automatically blaming yourself or making excuses for him/them.

<136>
Make A List Of All The Things You Want To Do Together

If you're traveling with your partner, it's essential to develop a list of things that both partners want. It may be hard at first, but this will make everything easier.

<137>

Discuss What Is And Isn't OK For Each Person

Each individual in the relationship has different needs. Some personal boundaries should never be crossed.

<138>

Plan Trips Around Both Your Interests

Planning a trip where both partners enjoy the activities that are designed can have a better outcome.

<139>
Create Your Bucket List Together

If you're discussing relationships, it's essential to discuss what each person wants out of life and see how they align.

<140>
Agree On An Itinerary For Your Trip So That There Are No Surprises

It's essential to plan a trip so that there are no surprises and should include both partners' interests. The itinerary can be designed with the knowledge of what will happen during each day. This also helps alleviate some anxiety for those who may worry about what they'll do when faced with new situations.

<141>
Plan Some activities with one another before you go, like cooking or watching movies together at night

Planning activities ahead of time helps to reduce the anxiety that may come with a new experience. It also allows people who are less experienced at something, like cooking or watching movies, an opportunity to learn in a low-pressure environment.

<142>

Cook Dinner For Each Other At Least Once A Week

Cook dinner for each other at least once a week. You don't need to be any kind of chef; you just need an interest in cooking and making food that's not always take-outs

This will show your partner that you care about them, which they'll appreciate on days when work is stressful, or things are tough.

<143>
Be Comfortable With Each Other's Company When Traveling Together

Be comfortable with each other's company when traveling together. This may seem obvious, but many people are more afraid of spending time alone than they would be flying in an airplane, even though the probability of dying while traveling is much higher.

<144>

Navigating Jealous Feelings With Your Partner Is Normal

Navigating jealous feelings with your partner is normal. It's important to discuss why you're feeling this way and talk about how they can fix it next time.

<145>
How Not To Be Jealous

It's pretty OK to be jealous sometimes--it shows your care, and we all know that some people are more caring than others. But if you want to know how not to be jealous, give personal attention and validation, express gratitude for what they provide in your life.

You can have a healthy relationship with jealousy by actually looking at what it is in a particular situation that makes you jealous--jealousy gives us just as much information about the kind of relationship we're trying to have as any other feeling or expression does. Becoming aware of its various meanings can go a long way towards making it helpful rather than dangerous; for instance, it can help you notice which areas of your life feel neglected or unappreciated.

<146>

When An Ex Is Back In Your Life or Theirs

When an ex comes into the picture, they have no place in your life.

Having a new person back at the office is annoying and distracting, which is why it's best to stifle that impulse of desire or curiosity. It won't take much time for you to recognize their quirks, faults, and why you broke up in the first place. Trust me on this one - so don't talk to them - avoid them through group setting if possible."

<147>
Being Each Other Cheerleader

Being in a relationship is hard, especially when the other person needs support. This can be difficult because we all have the demons that plague us every day; relationships are not immune to these traumas and tics. Sometimes it can feel like you're going through this battle alone, but if we learn how to love and support each other, we can both come out stronger.

<148>
Learning To Love Unconditionally

Yes, it's tough, but love is not about being perfect. It's about accepting the flaws and imperfections that make us who we are, as well as those of our partners. When you're in love, it should be a place where you feel safe enough to share all your thoughts and feelings without fear of judgment or criticism.

<149>

Understanding How Each Person Communicates

Everyone has a way they communicate with others; some people talk more while others prefer writing things down. Some like to text because it feels less intrusive than phone calls. In contrast, other couples find texting impersonal, so they only have conversations via telephone or face-to-face meetings instead. But these differences don't need to become issues if both parties know what makes the other.

FRIENDS/FAMILY WHILE IN A RELATIONSHIP

<150>
Introducing Your Partner To Your Family

It can be hard to introduce your partner to your family, but it's essential for both of you. It's a chance for them to get the opportunity to meet and talk about their future with each other."

<151>
Introducing Your Partner To Your Friends

This can be a little nerve-wracking because you want your friends to like them and vice versa. One thing that is important for when introducing a partner to friends, it's best they're not on their phone."

<152>
You Don't Veto Your Partner's Friends

You don't veto your partner's friends. This is a surefire way to cause resentment and will lead to the end of the relationship.

<153>
Make Time To See Your Friends Even In A New Relationship

It's essential to have your own time and be there for them as well. Being in a relationship doesn't mean you can't make plans with friends without the other person. It means that you should both want to spend some one-on-one time together just as much or more than spending it with outside people. Make sure you're not neglecting either of these relationships when in a new partnership!

<154>
Try To Find Common Ground With Them If Possible

If you are meeting their parents and have not supported the relationship, try to find common ground with them. This will make it easier for them to accept you as a part of the family because they won't feel like they sacrificed anything by being in this relationship.

<155>

Dress Appropriately, Avoid Wearing Revealing Clothing

Dress in something classy and straightforward, so you don't make their parents feel any more uncomfortable than they already are about meeting their son's girlfriend/daughter's boyfriend.

<154>

Make Sure To Be On Time, If Not A Little Earlier

It is essential to be on time, or even a little bit earlier. This shows respect and consideration for their parents' schedule, and it will show them that you are serious about this relationship.

<155>
Bring Gifts

If you're meeting your girlfriend/boyfriend's parents who have not supported the past, bring gifts when visiting them.

<156>

Don't Talk About Politics or Religion With Them

It is essential to know what you will not be discussing with them. If they're political people and have strong opinions on specific topics, it's best not to talk about those things so that the day goes smoothly.

<157>
Watch What You Drink

Drinks can be a great way to break the ice but don't overdo it. If you're going on a family dinner for people who are not used to drinking, have only one drink so that they'll feel comfortable.

<158>
Be Mindful Of Your Words And Actions

When meeting new parents, always remember: You never know what someone has experienced in the past. Humor can be a great way to break the ice but always take things into context.

<159>
Be Polite And Use Proper Manners

Regardless of your beliefs or knowledge, it's best not to show off when meeting people for the first time. A good rule is that if you want them to like you, then make sure they feel comfortable around you.

<160>
Don't Talk Too Much About Yourself

Everyone has their own life, and what is best for you may not be the same thing as someone else. Remember that relationships are about give-and-take.

MONEY IN A RELATIONSHIP

<161>
How to Handle Money in a Relationship

Money is always tricky to tackle in relationships, but the couple must agree on how the funds will be handled and spent. It can be hard when one person wants to spend more than the other or put their own needs before each others' because they feel like there isn't enough money, so discuss this as soon as possible!

<162>
Avoid Those That Are Bad With Money

One of the most important lessons that one can learn in a relationship is handling money properly. Many people are financially irresponsible, and if this person happens to be your significant other, they will likely do things like spend all their money on clothes or neglect paying bills altogether.

This may not seem like it's such an issue at first, but once your bank account gets depleted, then it's an issue.

It is essential only to date people who are responsible for the money.

- Do not spend all their money on clothes.
- Pay bills on time
- Saving some for emergencies and unexpected expenses
- I was only buying what they can afford at the moment, no shopping sprees or going into debt over a purchase just because someone wanted it.

BEING SINGLE

<163>

What To Do When You're Feeling Lonely And Single

It's OK to feel lonely and single at times, but it can be an excellent time to take care of yourself when you're feeling like this. It may sound cliche, but the best thing you can do is find something for yourself that will make you happy or go out with your friends.

Don't let being on your own make you feel less worthy or like a failure.

<164>
Why You Should Never Settle For Less Than What You Deserve

Don't settle for anything less than what you deserve. You are worthy of love and should be with someone who respects you, loves you, cares about your feelings and treats you how they want to be treated in a relationship.

<165>
Be OK With Being Single

You might have to be OK with being single at times. "It's a new way of life," says Loeschner. You're not always going to feel like you want someone around."

"Being an adult and being in a relationship can get tricky, but there are ways to navigate the waters well! Some ground rules for being single are not to date anyone who is in a relationship, and always watch over yourself."

"Remember: being an adult doesn't mean you're all alone. You can be happy with someone but sometimes on your own too!"

<166>
The Benefits Of Being Single

Being single can be great! You get to spend all your time doing what you love, whether that's alone or with friends.

The best thing about being single is that you get to have more time for yourself. You can travel, try new activities and go on adventures without anyone else needing your attention.

There are no commitments, and you can be yourself without having to worry about upsetting the other person or keep a secret from them. You have your own time, space, and privacy at all times because you don't have to report back to anyone.

<167>
How To Be Happy When You're Single

There are things you can do to make being single a lot more fun. You can learn interesting facts about people and places, visit places that have meaning for you or help your community, volunteer or donate your time.

Go out and meet new people, especially when you're not dating anyone. This is a great way to make friends who you can talk to about your interests and hobbies and be there for you without any distractions.

www.ingramcontent.com/pod-product-compliance
Lightning Source LLC
Chambersburg PA
CBHW061324040426
42444CB00011B/2770